waterways series

At Damascus Gate on Good Friday

releasing new voices, revealing new perspectives

At Damascus Gate on Good Friday

waterways
an imprint of flipped eye publishing
www. flippedeye.net

First Edition
Copyright © Agnes Meadows, 2005
Cover Image © Agnes Meadows, 2005
Cover Design © flipped eye publishing, 2005

ISBN-1-905233-00-0

To my wonderful family in Gaza, who have given me so much love and appreciation. I love you all.

At Damascus Gate on Good Friday

At Damascus Gate on Good Friday

Contents

While Reading Eliot at the Beach Hotel (Gaza)

Silver loaded sea frets and stumbles,
Slow as an old man running on the waiting shore;
Sky tosses itself, a pewter disc skeined with melting
Copper threads, all the way to Venus and back.

It will rain tonight,
Or so the fingering feather clouds tell me,
And my nose itches with unborn cumulus,
Alert to the coming shower's thrash.

Boats hover in the crumbling harbour
Shifting from place to place
Like the feet of enamoured fishermen.
They cannot leave her alone, this wild
Woman ocean with her broken teeth
And coral eyes. They cannot live without her.

The jetty clamours with dark-skinned men
All dying of love, walking back and forth
In madness, useless as last year's harvest
That has perished on the stalk.

God seems very close tonight,
Joining air to water with invisible stitches,
Throwing old ruby sun into her dark bed
With a light hand. Her dreams firework upwards

Into a thousand scarlet chrysanthemums, crimson
Wreaths and poppies stretching endlessly ahead.

I have never seen anything like it.

The Dreaming of Children

They dream of stillness,
Of hop-scotch afternoons and dusty dabka dancing.

They dream of listening to how things grow
Of grasses rustling taffeta ears by empty roadsides,
Slow clambering up from waiting earth to worm-turn
                                   eagerness.

They dream of ripe food smells soft-crawling from the plate,
Of aubergine love and green olive consummation,
The scent of tangerines knife-sharp at four p.m.
Bread stealing hunger, and rumbling belly laughs.

They dream of prayers filled only with bus rides and bicycles,
School-days passing in a blur of hands and feet,
Markets,
Minarets,
Marriage days,
Eyes stacked high with promises,
The rolling sway of girls raising dust and longing
As they walk, bride-price passion not far away,
Another year… perhaps two
(Insh'Allah – If God wills it).

They dream of God's breath bejewelling each cheek,
Faith's opulence giving them colour and balance,

Giving Hope another coin-flick chance,
Another roll of the dice,
Gambling on justice,
6/6 – double figures.

This time, next time, some time, maybe....
They dream of winning.

Keith and I on the Balcony (Tel Aviv)

We sat on his balcony, air still brisk
With April's slow ripening, jets competing with stars
To fill the night sky, two old friends
Band-aiding each other's memories.

We talked about emotions, rejection, denial,
Past and present loneliness, each day
An act of heroism by virtue of its completion.

He drank too much, became voluble,
Augmenting his generosity with tears.
I laughed too loud, wishing I could unwrap
Happiness once more outside of birthdays.

We both skirted fear
Whose wolverine jaws snapped silent as moonlight
Waiting to eat us up raw.

His lover, unthawed, had perfected self-containment;
Mine was far away, beyond un-crossable borders.

We shared tales of love at a distance,
Arms-length love which gave little
While promising everything.

Its wounds bit very deep.

No Ordinary Gift

No ordinary gift, I send you a sky
Full of stars and a quiet sea.

Silence, like a lover's kiss at midnight, with the world waiting.
My skin, golden with promise under your hand.
Pleasure quenching thirst, a stream of silver
On your tired body, life passing power
Through the never-ending kiss.

Out in the darkness, memory of firelight warms your fingers.
Saffron Autumn leaves edged in frost knee-deep
On the October ground. The smell of the banquet lays thick,
wine's laughter pouring from the flask, fear turned away,
No beggar at the feast of your life.

Better than law and temperance, soft words lightly spoken,
My eyes, like a lake in the morning, there for your soul's
                                        breathing,
With white blossoms a-stippling the path, and wild lilies
Hemming the water's edge, birdsong and bells seam the
                                        yellow afternoon,
Crickets hidden in long grasses, time languid as a lazy cat.

On gorse-covered hillsides, rain dances like a young girl
Caught up in passion, pleasure in each step taken,
Joy in her jewelled fingers of memory, alight as candles

Gracing your eyes. My mouth, honeyed with longing, marks
Your shadow-bruised flesh, a slow mist arising through

The ocean's rasp before we sleep.
No ordinary gift I send you.

Are These Daffodils?

"Are these daffodils?" he asked,
White and purple flowers clustered in his hands,
A gift of love on this uncompromising February night.

He had little knowledge of Spring's soft curling stretch
From buds stitched like buttons onto the unclothed fingers of
                                                    trees,
Knew nothing of Gaia's gestating whisper of vernal adoration,
A crescendo of resurrected hope unfreezing each ice-checked
                                                    soul.

Where he came from, seasons did not drift in harmonious
                                                    quartets
Across the knit of chanting hills,
But leapt in steel-capped boots one to another,
Swiftly,
Laying everything bare,
Burning to the bone.

Where he came from, love had become a forgotten song
Stolen by an alien conductor,
Then bludgeoned to submission.

Yet, love had made him proud,
Had wounded him in the uneasy democracy of betrayal,
Cradled him for decades, gifting him both hunger and
                                                    fulfilment,

Stamped him with an identity that could never be erased.

He carried this legacy of love,
Dormant and undying,
Flickering in his eyes like Pacific Neons,
A miraculous shoal of emotions
Alight with a warmth tonight's London winter cannot
                                    extinguish.

Now it was offered to me,
Not easily,
But with the bashful hesitation of decades unfenced in his
                                    glance,
His whole life on his sleeve,
A patchwork life tailored with priceless eloquence.

To him all flowers were equal,
An inconsequential Valentine's attestation.
But now, each time I see lemon mouths shrieking 'Spring' at
                                    ankle height,
I will remember his question,
And know
On that night,
I was loved.

East Jerusalem Nightfall

Suleiman Street slows down its heartbeat,
Old City walls slumber through secrets,
Their pale blonde stones exhaling centuries of exchange.
A dignity so profound it is tangible among the dirty trees
Embraces everything that moves
Leaves men speechless.
Buses roll by empty;
Children tiptoe;
Even dogs fail to bark, looking over their shoulders at
                                    collecting night,
A little nervous, tails a-twitch.
One by one the stars give us sleep,
The gold-domed eye rolls closed,
Dreaming sets in,
And moths begin to fingerprint the lowering light,
Dusting threadbare earth with frail bronzed wings.

New Year's Day

Jabalia Refugee Camp, Gaza

Post Eid visiting has begun.
Generations of women sit cross-legged
In bare January's leaf-strewn inner courtyard
Consuming dates, coffee, scandal, memories.

In one corner,
Darbuka's forgotten celebration notes still lingering,
Oblivious to watching eyes,
A trio of girls not yet ten dances in pale blonde sunlight,
Like multi-coloured mid-day moths.
Meringued in lace, tinselled to within an inch of their lives.

They pirouette unsmiling,
Heart-shaped Hollywood shades covering honey eyes,
Totally intent,
Repressing unseemly laughter,
Spreading their wings,
Testing their strength.

And, elsewhere,
Plump Tarik makes more tea,
Plotting fraternal revenge
At being left out.

On the Beach at Gaza

On a golden chain
I wear a mottled shell
Rounded smooth by years of wave-kiss,
Brown as early raisins, white as feta in winter.
It carries sea-shore memory,
Plucked from the damp sand on one small day of joy.

Boys cart-wheeled through layered tidal flotsam,
Spinning with firework ebullience,
Bare-legged and tattered.
I snatched their shouting,
Held it to my ear, caught in my clenched fist,
Fastened, please-pleeeeeazzing
Like a brilliant buzzing fly.

We ate cheese, chick-peas, flat bread factory leavened.
They tasted of freedom,
Warm friendships,
Thoughts of tea ripe with sage as dusk drew closer.

We laughed at
Anything, every, everything,
While we still had time,
While we still could.

I carved a fish in the sand,

Watched it swim away from me like a slippery dream,
Back to Neptune's touch
And the kiss of mermaids diving far out at sea
Beyond where gun-ships rattle.

Oasis

I sit behind the latticed windows
Watching dawn's light, pale as seashells, crease the Eastern
                                                    sky,
Morning rising from uneasy sleep upon a thousand window
                                                    sills,
Air fresh as new washed sheets.

He will be here soon, and I can begin to breathe again.

This is my sanctuary of stillness,
This time of anticipation,
The pause between notes in the music of his presence,
His eyes, when smiling, a library of knowledge,
Each hand's touch a poem waiting for the unwritten page.

If I close my eyes
I can see him weaving through the early traffic,
Curving past city doorways,
Blind to the unlit windows of empty-desked offices,
Telephones cradling their heads on still slumbering arms,
Their dreams innumerate and voiceless.

Shopkeepers yawn and stumble into the arms of another day,
Greeting commerce like an unwelcome wife,
Despised but necessary.
He hails each one by name,

Calling out "Sabah kherim – May God grant you a generous
morning",
Laughing even when they turn away
Gray and grumbling.

He stops to drink coffee
So thick and sweet it could start wars,
Sees our future joined in the grounds,
The battle of separation finally finished.
It makes me smile to imagine such a thing.

On the roof of our house, my Mother grows roses in oilcans,
A blazing masquerade of scarlet and butter yellow.
Sometimes I hear them whispering floral secrets
On warm summer evenings
When the moon floats on the untroubled flood of paradise.
They join our names in this clandestine mystery of love,
Holding their knowledge of us away from the world.

He has promised me a garden of my own
Where I can listen to growth second by second,
The insignificant creak of petals unfurling,
The waiting earth turbulent with life.

I have promised him an orchard of sons,
A serenity of daughters,
A lifetime of unblemished mornings
Each one a harbour to us.

Red Onions

My sparrow-spring girl is crying again, not silently,
With the precocious dignity of those old before their time,
But with noisy, terrified tears as befits an 8-year-old
Who has just seen her best friend murdered before her eyes.

Her weeping splits apart the fabric of evening,
A grey cotton shroud torn to bitter shreds,
A wailing siren of grief shaking the walls of her home
Like an angry robber intent on stealing midnight's stillness.

This vibrant, joyful, dancing child,
Who turned me around with her laughter,
Spun me like a top until I became dizzy with love,
Now shouts and trembles, convulsing with torment,
Beats her father in blind uncomprehending rage,
Her small fists nailing stations of the cross upon his flesh.

He smokes too many cigarettes, becomes absorbed in the
                                        mending
Of clocks, radios, other broken things, a family joke
That seems to have lost its punch line, for his child cannot be
                                        fixed
Tonight, a clockwork toy that has been wound up once too
                                        often,
Spitted by a soldier's sniping savagery.

She has been undone by horror, unravelled by memories of
                                    blood
Splashed with geranium freshness onto the fearful ground.

Her brothers hold her close
As if by doing so they will absorb her anguish,
Join up the circle of her broken heart,
Rekindle the flame of innocence within her.

Her mother occupies herself in the kitchen,
Holding things together with soup,
Slivers of chicken,
Eggplant, green peppers.

It is the red onions that make her eyes water,
Nothing more.
Just the red onions.

Sarah Behind Glass

(Nablus)

Sarah behind glass,
Fragile as a window-pane, eight years old
And buzzing in life's high intensity,
A coin thrown up into the air, a drumbeat,
A gamble of joy, a soft rock pressing
Her fingers against the hard place of possibility.
She watches the world with old woman eyes,
Grandmother eyes replete with generations of woe,
Soaked with half a century of loss.
Only an echo of childhood remains like a ghost
Playing in a long abandoned ruin,
Wandering through empty rooms, wailing
With loneliness, transparent with longing.

Fear has stretched her tight,
Tight as a drum, fright growing
Like bindweed, slowly, inexorably,
Covering everything,
Making ordinary things unrecognisable,
Making her dreams noisy and terrible,
A reflection of terror, a broken mirror
Whose splinters show fragments of her,
As if she had already been shattered by war.

Breath stuck in his throat like a guilty bone,
Her father attempts reassurance.

She no longer believes him.
Secretly he acknowledges safety is no longer an option,
He cannot protect her or heal her wounds,
Cannot kiss the sore place,
Cannot take away the night-hag hunters,
Cannot make it better.
These things are no longer possible.
The days when he was king to her princess are gone,
For gunfire has replaced reason, turmoil
Has supplanted love. His child has old woman eyes,
And nothing will ever be the same.

Sarah behind glass,
Remembers yesterday's birthday party,
Cake trampled in the rush to be safe from mortar fire.
Bullets enter her home like uninvited guests,
Leaving a trail of angry desolation. None tagged with her
                                    name
Today, though tomorrow might tell a different tale.

Exposure

Al Ahzar University, Gaza

She was a phantom, a raven,
A shadow, silent and skimming
Burka'd so deep even her soul was hidden,
Black cloth covered from head to heel, gloved
Hands like mummifed birds, feet trapped
In leather cages keeping pavements and earth at bay,
Not one inch of her revealed, not the smallest
Flicker of flesh free to feel life's firmament.

She slid across the ground, leaving no trace,
Stateless in Gaza, coffined already,
Walking through life in a box, a black box, a shroud,
Heart beat and being's treasured threads concealed,
Arcane messages Morse-coding out of spectral irises.

She glided into the classroom, de-humanised,
Mute and removed, devoid of identity,
Surrounded by youth's questioning tidal wave,
Yet separate, a black shore upon which no wave would ever
                                        beat,
In her cerecloth covering, a ghost, a djinn,
Conjured out of midday heat, then vanishing
Between one sentence and the next, gone, dimmed,
Disappearing back into the lamp without so much as a
                                        goodbye.

It saddened me that I would never know her name,
Not hear her breathing, know her thoughts, share
Her acknowledgement of pride, victory of laughter,
Softness of pleasure when the sea brakes, when the rain
                                        comes,
Discover if she was a woman worth knowing as a friend.

And ultimately I wondered if she pitied me
For my complete
Exposure.

Silent Conversations

I have seen poems written on the palms of women's hands,
Silent conversations
In which fury is hidden
And passion veiled.

'Oh love,' say the fingers,
'Let me touch your face, set you free.
You are a martyr lost in the forest.
You cannot find your way home
And I cannot seek you,
For I am locked behind walls and promises,
Separated by glass and grief
And the demands of a lesser god.

'I am forced to breed martyrs
Whose blood rages on hostile pavements.
I see their faces contorted with despair
The theatre of rage acted out before my eyes.

'My children lie scattered around me,
Split open like ears of corn half consumed by ravens,
The fire of their lives blown out.
I am expected to be grateful, proud of the death
Of my offspring. I am not allowed
To express my sorrow or weep in public.
It is a sign of weakness, they say.

'I must turn my face back into the wilderness
As if nothing had happened,
Return to silence, sit quietly in shadows,
My world shrunk to rooms instead of continents.
My spirit shrivels away from feeling. My heart turns
To wood ready for burning,
To stone ready for transport.

'I wear my tomorrows like cheap tin
Baubles, which have lost their shine,
Tarnished and thinned with constant use.
I am allowed nothing else.

'My dreams go unrecognised,
Cut up and thrown to the four winds,
Scattered beyond the simple barriers
With which I am surrounded standing
Like a dunce, with my face to the wall,
Seeing nothing, hearing nothing, saying nothing.
I have lost the knack of pleasure.
I have lost the habit of joy.'

There are poems written on the faces of women.
'Oh love,' say the eyes,
'I am a willow bending under your glance.
Look away, lest you are discovered
And they send you from here.
We will both be exiled, we will both suffer.
Look away. We will keep our humanity secret.
I will pretend I do not know you,
And when the time is right I will

Bear you only sons, for my daughters have
Been removed already from this life, censored,
Become mad with grief.

This will never pass.
This will never be recognised.'

Waiting for Attack

In the garden of the British Council, Gaza City.

A faded back-street garden
Replete with millennial clutter;
A day warm as baking bread,
Comfortable as sun-porch seating.

An almond tree continues to blossom,
Its petals pink as children's fingernails,
Roses forget their exhaustion,
Yawning and stretching in February bud,

And schools of bees tread this year's pollen vintage,
Stumble and seethe along the branch,
Then zzzzzzzzzag back to troubled hives,
Blind and burdened. Soon there will be honey.

Ants perforate the concrete path with their single-line poetry,
Driven by the instinctive syllables of birth, reproduction,
                                        death,
In strict obedience to their dark-nest Queen.

The sun thaws red brick walls, unfurling lemon grass,
Chattering sparrow fledglings, and clouds curl round
Geese arrowing north again,
An SOS of wings morse-coding their journey home.

Every single thing is in its place.
Every single thing is at it should be according to Gaia's plan.
On such a smooth, unruffled day, breathing seems easy.

It's then you become aware
That you have been holding your breath
In anticipation of attack;
You become aware that you have been waiting
For the next round of conflict;
You become aware that you have been watching
The sky unknowing,
And your eyes are tired of the memory of destruction.

And waiting is the worst thing of all.

They're Bombing the Port Again *at Gaza*

Explosions blossom in the Khamseen darkness
Like bloodied chrysanthemums of sound.
Dogs begin howling, an orchestra of woe;
Cockerels roar in pre-dawn confusion;
Crickets start to creak in shock.
Only the people are silent, to weary even to stir
From their beds, accustomed to this lullaby of conflict.

It had been an ordinary day.
At the Palestine Hotel I had seen a wedding
And wished it were my own.
The bride moved like a clockwork meringue
Through a gleeful, clapping throng.
The groom had a plastic smile hammered to his face,
Genuine fear turning his features wooden.

On the radio, a woman had wept for her imprisoned son.
He'd been going to market, nothing more dangerous
Than a bag of tomatoes in his hand,
But they'd arrested him anyway
(Something to do to fill the day!).
Her desperation poured itself onto the airwaves,
Voice twisting and turning, a knife in a million hearts.
Hers is a common tale; broken hearts are a common
Currency in Gaza, debased, devalued and worthless

On the global market, thousands to a pound or dollar.

People with nothing left to give still offered me the gift of
                                                        welcome,
An honourable giving, smiles chasing me down the
                                                        beachfront,
Through grey be-littered squares where despondency squatted
like hoary grandfathers, shrivelling in the sun,
A shimmering mirage, like young men's dreams.
Clusters of brown-eyed boys followed me
Along the sandy street shouting "Hello London",
Grinning and leaping with pleasure when I replied
In Arabic "Marhaba shebab" –
Half my vocabulary used up in seconds.

And at no time
During that glow-ball juggling day
Did I feel
Endangered.

That came later when at 2.00 a.m.,
Safely tucked up in my bed,
They started bombing the Port again
At Gaza.

The Man Who Died in the Pursuit of Freedom

Death changes everything. Love becomes a net,
Through which emotions wriggle, yearning for escape.
We forget the concept of pleasure, forget the hunger of
                                        waking,
The resonance of gravity binding hunter to hunted
In the unending symbiosis of opposites.

> *In Gaza after the attack he lays on the ground surrounded by*
> *   carnage*
> *Feeling the doorway to eternity creak open beneath him,*
> *No longer capable of feeling pain.*
> *He watches dust motes struggle in the sunlight,*
> *Each one containing a universe of thought, dancing like a*
> *   leaf,*
> *A red kite, fingers of wind tugging against constraint.*

In such moments of intensity only the microcosm remains;
The mind slams shut, emotional extremity's trip-switch
Thrown to guard against the threat of drowning,
Small moments in a chain of triviality,
Tiny tears that scar the moving dust,
Nothing worth noting in a day's passage,
Everything, and nothing.

Too much death makes us contemptuous of life,

Makes us forget to give thanks for this evolutionary gift,
Spitting in the face of God with obscene disregard for
miracles....
(A smile requires 15 facial muscles to work in tandem.)
(The human heart beats 130,000 times a day, a million times a
week.)
(The Greeks acknowledged there were four different types of
love.)

In Gaza he lays on the ground ebbing away.
He will be gone soon,
But for now he continues to measure his remaining seconds
Watching the sky unravel into dusk,
Remembering his wife's eyes,
Weddings,
　　Friendships,
　　　　Graduation,
　　　　　　Family,
　　　　　　　　Birth,
Familiar things ribboning past instantaneously full circle
into time...

(Agape, Philios, Eros and Praxis,
The Greeks acknowledged there were four different types of
love.)

And in Gaza he forgets his dreams,
Forgets his name,
Forgets dimension and place.
The name of his jailor escapes him.
Another outcast from Paradise, he remembers only Philios,
The humanity of brothers; his unquenchable longing for home.

His body transforms to a garden of chrysanthemums
Blossoming freely where once his heart had pumped,
Their scarlet petals spreading over the earth
Leaving no shadow, making no sound.

He has become no more than a breath in the mouth of God

At Damascus Gate on Good Friday

Above dam-bursts of unruly trade;
Above scarlet scented strawberries which ripen afternoon
                                        prayers,
Or apples hard as diamonds fearing the intruding bite,
Or peaches too young for picking, still holding blossom
                                        memory;
Above the anarchy of flies dancing in jagged arabesque;
Above rosaries of pilgrims chaining back to their invisible
                                        saviours,
Skeins of Ethiopian nuns, or Filipino faithful,
Or pale northern Christians, bemused and badly dressed;
Above all these things there hangs a city
Where domed chimneys thrust up like old Astarte's breasts,
And windows mosaic between unravelling tattered rooftops
Half exposing small daily truths
Hidden shyly behind grey wooden shutters,
Watching, unrepentant, a nation
Being crucified.

Broken Glass

Night falls in dirty old London.
Neon logos pierce the weight of history,
A stone's throw of temporal architecture slumbering in ancient
                                        bricks and mortar
And overlaid with the mossy graffiti of centuries.

Buses rumble by, growling and grumbling like worn out lions,
Splashing you with urban jungle grime, and taxis prowl the
City's arteries
Snatching folk off trash-grey streets as if they were
                                        kidnapping brides
Held to ransom by unromantic brigands.

A spiteful wind slices all the way from Shadwell basin,
Bank-side trees turning their backs on November,
Shrugging softness off their branches,
Leaving nothing but bare bones shaking their fists skyward.

A carpet of beggars cough and rattle under railway arches,
Wild-eyed women whose children have all died,
Their gentleness leached away by barefoot, tumbled men
                                curling like eddies of leaves in
        doorways marked EXIT,
A fitting epitaph for those laid waste within this hungry civic
                                        wasteland.

Even Old Father Thames is tired tonight,
Tug boats sluggish with effort, oiling up water with pig-iron
                                            strain.
It's been a long time since fish swam in this river,
Even the memory of fish long drowned.

Tonight everyone walks in couples unaware of the riches they
                                            display,
Taking tenderness for granted,
Kissing carelessly under street lamps,
A casual marriage of moth and lamp that mocks my inability
                                            to touch.

And I, missing you,
Am branded by loneliness
Harsh as broken glass
Sharding my soul.

Life Fall

Take a leaf
Broken by November's somnolent fear.
Watch it sieve to the pavement
Hand-printing the air with mellow ruined fingers,
Then congregate in gutters,
Settle in doorways with a million brothers,
A dying tribe of plane and sycamore wrapped for comfort in
                                        old newsprint,
Scuttle round corners on crackling, crumbling tip-toes,
Rolling and rattling like russet dice thrown in challenge to the
East wind.

And winter is a-coming,
The goose becomes fat with fright,
Hiding its neck, feathers thicker than iron knives,
Wishes it was thin again
As in the lemon-lit days of summer,
Life stretching ahead unfettered by seasonal feasting,
And the way south still a harmonious possibility.

Apples fall from the bough,
Rouged and roguish,
Strike the ground like bells without clappers
Tock...
            Tock...

Tock…
They have the secret of the Lady hidden in their hearts,
Initials of unnamed husbands concealed beneath their skin
Waiting to be undressed,
Teasing smiles from the lips of merry maidens who dance on
the Sabbath
Become foolish with honeyed mead and dreams fermented in
the cask.

Come Jack-o-Lantern,
Come Willow-the-Wisp,
Come smile your flickering smile,
Bite the earth with your ragged teeth until the Green Man
bleeds.
Forget instruction and tradition,
Burn candles at midnight, their smoke matching moonlight,
Watch the Wild Hunt hurl itself, shaking and clattering, from
the breaching hillsides
Into the world of men.

The Old Woman opens Her arms in welcome,
Hair ripe with mistletoe and holly berries,
Scalding human hearts on the open flame of Midwinter kisses.
Soon She will be scythed into submission,
Laced to the drowsing earth by invisible filaments of frost and
February,
Her laughter no louder than leaf fall.

Jerusalem Afternoon

Coffee stiff with cardamom;
Tamarind in rose-red sweetness;
Shop doorways crowded
With all the paraphernalia of Arabesque,
And the dusty percussion of young boy smiles;
White rock wasteland layered with cypresses
Carrying the memory of water, and Khaledh's eyes,
Liquid in sticky-toffee greeting,
Chin trembling with two-year-old doubts.
In a land of stones, sand and insults
Every surface writhes with flowers,
Mature and peacock brilliant,
Yet artificial as a politician's promises.

Gaza Wedding

Nuseirat Refugee Camp, Gaza

Suddenly from out of the dust and squalor,
A waterfall of children ran shrieking
Down the rubbled street towards me,
Shrieking and giggling,
Eyes filled with astonishment and laughter, a hundred
Hands reaching out, fingers fastening onto promises
My presence pledged, greedy for contact, hungry
To be recognised, each touch an open door,
Each smile a growing garden, each welcome
An oasis in this wilderness of separation.

It was impossible not to laugh with them,
Their hilarity contagious, and I was carried
Like a boat upstream on that river of merry children,
Today's joy a special gift costly as any bridal dowry.
They swept me forward over the grey earth,
Leaf-weak in the face of such happy strength,
Rafting into the wedding whirlpool, lifting me
Into its maelstrom, a storm of arms held high in celebration,
With the singing and the clapping coming in volleys,
Drumbeats sharp as bullets drowning me,
So that I became an island, a single tree, a sunflower
Alone in that jubilant flood.

I was given babies to hold, damp and decorated

As Christmas trees, their exclamation mark stares
Plucking at my crimson mouth.
The groom, shy in his new suit, encircled me
With cautious care, his mother, ululating pride,
Holding me in her hennaed hands as if I was precious.
Torrents of bold young men eddied around me, insistent,
Unshakable, relentlessly male, alive to the last
Heartbeat, curious, and wanting to know more,
Though this was not the time for asking.

For just one moment I was part of that community
Of gladness,
Linked to them despite betrayals
And the machinery of conflict.
Nothing coming next
Can scar
Or change that.

Hind

She butterflied into my life
Showering me with kisses
Turning around, round and around,
Turning around, round, round and around.
With her pixie-mischief eyes,
With her 'up-to-no-good' eyes,
With her 'it-wasn't-me-honest' eyes glinting,
And turning around, round and around,
Turning around, round, round and around,
Her 'stream-over-stones' laughter landing
On my cheek like wild flower petals,
Thistledown, buttercup, cuckoo-pint, ladies' fingers,
Rainbow girl, gossamer girl, turning my heart
Around, round and around, turning my heart
Around, round, round and around, green leaf girl,
Sparrow Spring girl, darting forward into trap-door April,
Hands ambushing every breathing moment
At full throttle, snatching ragged seconds,
Tearing up pages of life,
Squandering days of pleasure
With the generosity of childhood,
With the recklessness
Of not-yet-seven, and turning Hope around,
Round and around, turning Hope around,
Round, round, and around,
Yea…turning Hope
Round, round and around, round, round, and around…

Horse Whisperer

Birzeit, Palestine

Abu Mahanad, the horse whisperer, sits shy
In moth-dance darkness, his presence sign-posting
Life's romantic yesterday's, the old ways,
Out-dated as honour, fading now to sepia monochrome.

He has wilderness eyes, pale as the earth he ploughs,
Unfettered, like lightning striking grey ground,
Storm-furrow eyes, exposing painful truths,
Fearful and wriggling under such brutal light.

He has taken horses, unbroken,
Led them with his voice alone across the stones.
And they, mad with thirst, fearful of chains and bondage,
Have followed willingly, their hooves, like the feet of girls,
Weaving stencil tracks across bleached, layered hills,
Blowing their breath into his mouth as a sign of adoration.

He has taken children, sons and daughters, loosed them
Like sky-larks into the clouds, watched them soar
And swoop, a job well done,
A freedom worth waiting for.

Now grown, they write him guilty letters
From their sky-scrapered new world, longing
To replace his wilderness with Wall Street,

Finger-printing his sandstone face with biblical mythologies,
Seeing only impoverishment, an old man in a dusty suit,
Living on the bare earth with a dream-broken horse.

Solicitous, pleading, they have forgotten
His whispering. How he smiles at each furrow's start,
How he watches the horizon with silent pride,
His horizon, *his* Homeland.

Despite love, they are deaf to him, blinded
By betterment, mute to his soul's landscape,
The leaving of which would unravel his daily purpose
Killing him quicker than dispossession.